# WOW: Robots

## A Book of Extraordinary Facts

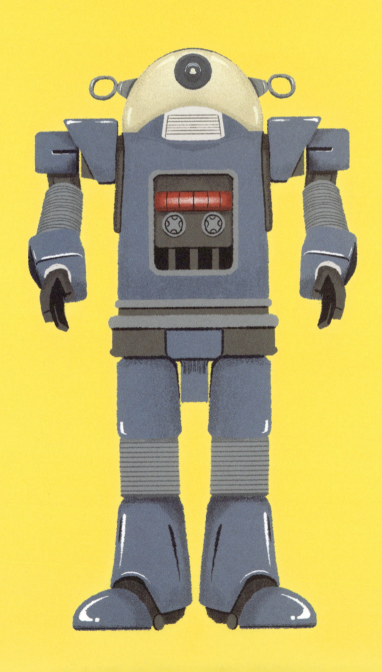

First published 2020
This edition published in 2023 by Kingfisher
an imprint of Macmillan Children's Books
The Smithson, 6 Briset Street, London, EC1M 5NR
Associated companies throughout the world
www.panmacmillan.com

EU representative: 1st Floor, The Liffey Trust Centre,
117-126 Sheriff Street Upper, Dublin 1 D01 YC4

Author: Andrea Mills
Senior editor: Lizzie Davey
Design and styling: Liz Adcock
Jacket design: Liz Adcock
Illustrations: Ste Johnson

ISBN 978-0-7534-4517-4

Copyright © Macmillan Publishers International Ltd 2020, 2023

All rights reserved. No part of this publication may be reproduced,
stored in or introduced into a retrieval system or transmitted, in any form
or by any means (electronic, mechanical, photocopying, recording or otherwise),
without the prior written permission of the publisher.

9 8 7 6 5 4 3
3TR/1123/WKT/UG/140WFO

A CIP catalogue record for this book is available from the British Library.

Printed in China

This book is sold subject to the condition that it shall not, by way
of trade or otherwise, be lent, resold, hired out or otherwise circulated without
the publisher's prior consent in any form of binding or cover other than that in which
it is published and without a similar condition including this condition being
imposed on the subsequent purchaser.

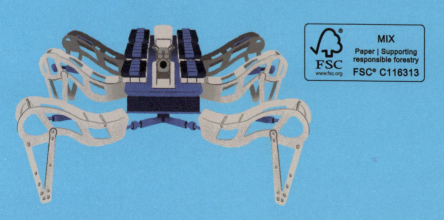

MIX
Paper | Supporting
responsible forestry
FSC® C116313

# WOW! Robots

## A Book of Extraordinary Facts

KINGFISHER

# Bring on the bots!

Robots can look like anything from a box to a person. Experts program robots to do what they want them to.

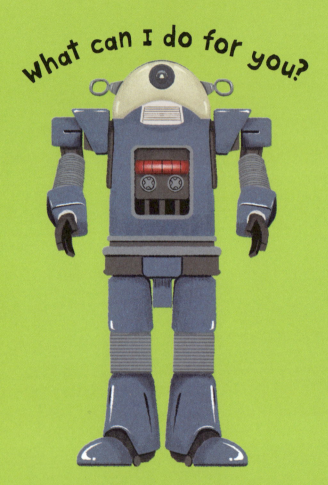

*What can I do for you?*

Bots are hard at work all over the world. They can do boring jobs or brilliant jobs – and everything in between. Some robots do the same thing again and again on factory production lines. Others do totally amazing things such as going into disaster zones or even into space!

**Robots range from seriously big bots to mini machines...**

The world's biggest robot is Tradinno, a giant walking dragon. It stands as tall as three giraffes. Tradinno has huge wings and a massive tail. Best of all, it breathes fire!

## Did you know?

The most expensive robot money can buy is the Asimo humanoid. It costs more than £1.8 million.

*Stand clear!*

The world's smallest robot is RoboBee. This bot is based on a real-life bee. It can fly and also swim! This teeny-tiny robot is operated by remote control.

I'm the same size as a fly, but please don't swat me!

**Wow!** There are more than 10 million robots in the world today.

# Back to basics

**Back in ancient times, the biggest brainboxes were already dreaming up designs for the first basic bots.**

According to local legend, a massive mechanical man named Talos was created to protect the Greek island of Crete in about 700 BCE. The bronze giant was said to throw rocks at enemies and his hot breath set fire to invading ships!

*I am Talos!*

**Wow!** The first robot was invented more than 2000 years ago.

*Pigeon power!*

Greek maths whizz Archytas of Tarentum invented the world's first robot in 400 BCE. It was a flying pigeon made from wood and powered by steam. The pigeon flew the length of two football pitches before running out of steam.

## Listen to our sweet robotic music!

Arabic inventor Ismail al-Jazari mixed mechanics and music together in the 12th century. The result was a four-piece robotic orchestra that played music from a boat on a lake. Powered by water, the orchestra featured two drummers, a flute player and a harpist.

## I'm absolutely quackers!

### Did you know?

In the past people built fake robots, which only worked because they had other people hiding inside, pulling ropes to make them move.

Another birdie bot was built by French inventor Jacques de Vaucanson in 1739. His Digesting Duck was a gold-plated mechanical version of a real duck. It could flap its wings, eat food and even go for a poo!

# Under control

All robots feature computer programs, but with very different levels of control. Some robots are completely controlled by humans, others have more freedom.

Some robots are operated using a remote control, in the same way we use remote controls for televisions. The operator presses buttons to tell the robot what to do. The most popular remote-controlled robots are drones, which can take pictures and videos from up in the air.

what's it like up there?

## Wow!

The fastest drone is the DRL Racer X, which can fly at 289 kilometres per hour.

Autonomous robots can operate automatically. They work within a limited range, because they cannot make decisions outside of the programs they have been given. Examples include a factory robot that carries out repetitive work, or a chess-playing robot that chooses from a series of set moves.

Check mate!

Hello computer! What should I do today?

The brainiest bots are the AI crew. These are the very latest robots, with the power to think and act like real people. Of course, they are not truly alive, but have very advanced computer programs to make them seem that way.

# Working wonders

Robots are happy to work hard. Factories use worker bots to do boring jobs so people don't have to.

Imagine doing the same job again and again all day every day. It would be boring and hard to keep concentrating. Unlike us, robots don't feel tired, get distracted or make mistakes – and they never take a holiday!

*There must be a better way of doing this...*

## Did you know?

The word 'robot' means 'forced work' and was first heard in a Czech play in the 1920s.

*This arm comes in handy!*

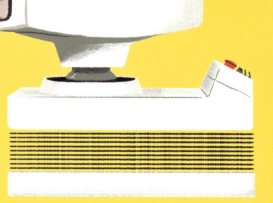

The first factory robots were simple machines programmed to do one basic task over and over again. American George Devol invented Unimate, a robotic arm with a gripper. This robot was programmed to move objects from one side of a room to another.

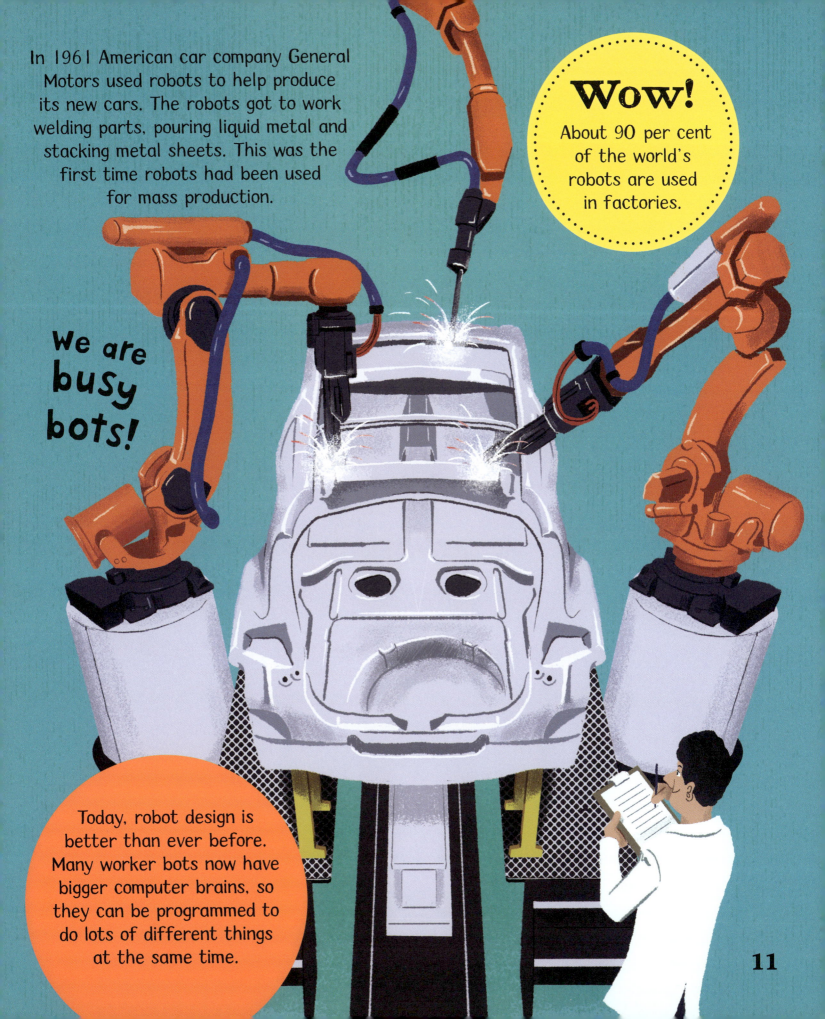

# Bot bits

Inside robots there are lots of bits and pieces. Most have many of the same essential parts.

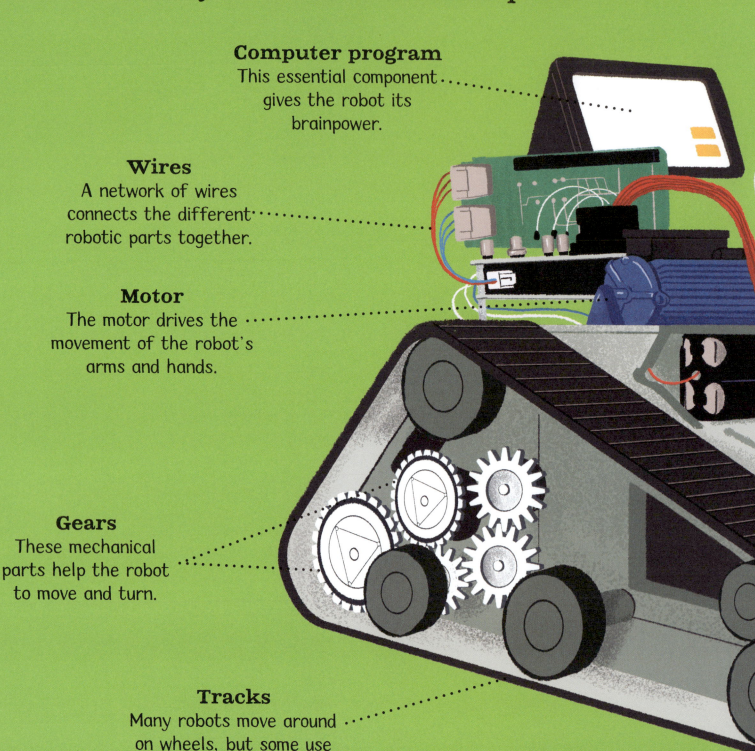

**Computer program**
This essential component gives the robot its brainpower.

**Wires**
A network of wires connects the different robotic parts together.

**Motor**
The motor drives the movement of the robot's arms and hands.

**Gears**
These mechanical parts help the robot to move and turn.

**Tracks**
Many robots move around on wheels, but some use legs or tracks, like these.

**Sensors**
The robot makes sense of its surroundings using sensors that respond to touch, temperature and pressure.

**Speakers**
Sounds can be sent out through speakers, giving the robot its own voice.

**Grippers**
The robot can grab hold of things without breaking them using hand-like grippers.

**Power supply**
Robots are usually powered by batteries or mains electricity.

**Lights**
Bright lights can show you if the robot is switched on, or help it be seen in the dark.

**Frame**
The body of the robot must be strong and supportive, and big enough to hold all the technology inside.

**Note**
This is just one example of a robot. Different gadgets and gizmos are used depending on what the robot is designed to do.

# Movers and shakers

**Robots are known for whizzing here, there and everywhere, but what gets them on the move?**

Just think how many bones, muscles and tendons you need to move around. Your body is a complex system, but your brain makes moving easy. Experts try to recreate our natural movements in robots, but it is very difficult.

Jointed elbow

Grippers

Rotating torso

## Wow!
Robots can work out how much pressure to put on different objects without breaking them.

Legs, wheels and tracks are all used for robot motion. Flexible, jointed legs, like ours, are the best solution to help robots cross bumpy terrain or climb stairs. If a robot needs to move quickly then wheels are the fastest option.

Jointed knees

## Wow!

The fastest legged robot in the world is Cheetah, which can reach speeds of 45 kilometres per hour.

## I'm wheelie good!

Mirra is a cleaning queen! This robot uses its wheels to power along swimming pool floors and remove dirt and debris from the water.

## Flying high!

Some robots are so advanced that they don't travel on land at all. Some take the plunge and swim through the water. Others can fly through the air to avoid obstacles on the ground.

## I'm a cheeky chimp!

The latest robots make it look easy! They can overcome obstacles and turn corners. This is Chimp. It is four times heavier than a real chimpanzee, and can walk on two or four limbs. Chimp takes uneven surfaces, steep walls and even ladders in its stride.

# Helping hand

Robot helpers work in homes and hospitals to make life easier for everyone.

If you don't want to tidy your bedroom, get a robot to do it! Home-help robots are specially designed to do everyday jobs, including cleaning, cooking and shopping. A Japanese company has designed a robot to recognise mess and tidy up rooms.

*You missed a sock, bot!*

Moley's Robotic Kitchen is a set of robotic arms that can make a meal from start to finish, then clean up afterwards.

*Dinner is served!*

If your garden is looking more like a jungle, get Kobi on the case. This robot cuts grass and piles up leaves.

*I have green fingers!*

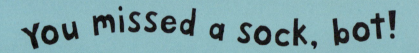

Robots are doing a good job in hospitals too. They make deliveries, help people with disabilities and even perform operations.

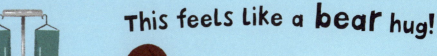

This feels like a **bear** hug!

Riba robot helps to lift hospital patients in and out of bed. To make things more fun, it looks like a bear!

I am Xenex...

...killer of germs!

King of cleaning, the Xenex robot zaps surfaces to kill germs. This hard work has led to fewer harmful infections in hospitals.

What next doc?

Surgical superstar Da Vinci performs operations on patients while doctors watch and control what is happening from three-dimensional (3D) screens.

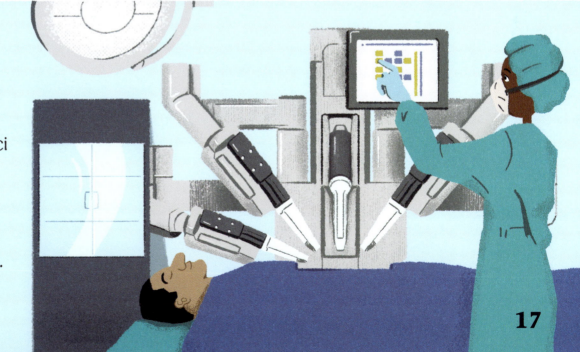

# Robotic welcome

Robots are running the show in airports, hotels and restaurants around the world. Ready to check in?

*Everyone smile for the camera...*

Pepper is about the same height as an eight-year-old child and provides services all over the place. It has taken orders in restaurants, been a tour guide in museums and worked as an assistant in shops. A screen on Pepper's tummy offers customer information and it always finds time to stop for a selfie!

*Hello, I'm GLAdys. Welcome to Scotland!*

**Wow!** Pepper can speak 15 languages!

A Pepper robot named GLAdys welcomes passengers to the departures desk at Glasgow Airport in Scotland. This happy humanoid has an information screen to help people find their way around the terminal. It also dances and sings songs.

# Making waves

**Whether diving down deep or scanning the surface, robots are working hard in our oceans.**

Spot something slippery in the sea? That's Eelume, the underwater bot that moves like an eel! This superb swimmer fixes off-shore oil rigs. It works in tight, dark places underwater that would be hard even for other robots to get to. Eelume uses specialist tools including camera and video equipment, depending on what the job involves.

*I stay underwater permanently, waiting for my next mission!*

Robot submarines carry out research deep in the oceans. Ships on the surface drop these subs to depths of 6000 m (19,500 ft) – far deeper than humans can reach. Robot submarines can stay underwater for many months because they have no crew on board.

**Wow!** Submarine bot Gavia explored the chilly waters beneath the Antarctic ice.

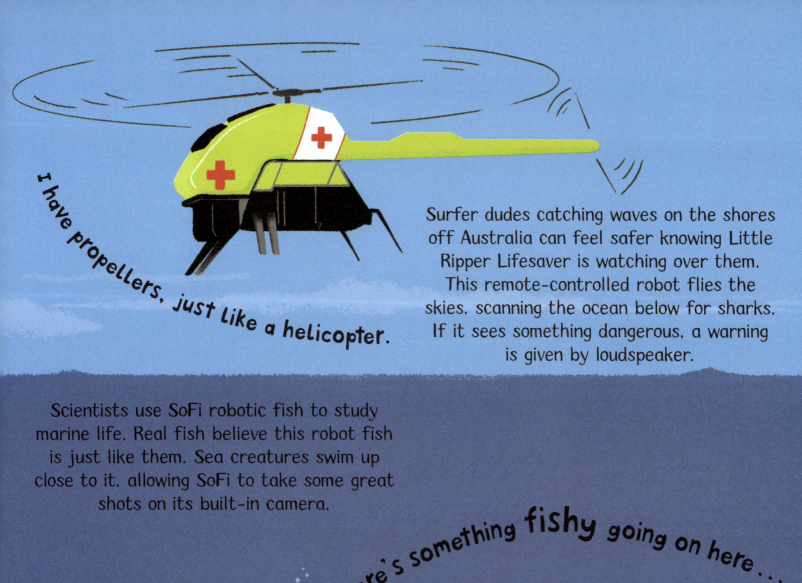

I have propellers, just like a helicopter.

Surfer dudes catching waves on the shores off Australia can feel safer knowing Little Ripper Lifesaver is watching over them. This remote-controlled robot flies the skies, scanning the ocean below for sharks. If it sees something dangerous, a warning is given by loudspeaker.

Scientists use SoFi robotic fish to study marine life. Real fish believe this robot fish is just like them. Sea creatures swim up close to it, allowing SoFi to take some great shots on its built-in camera.

There's something fishy going on here...

# Robot rescue

Emergency! Disaster areas can be too dangerous for people to enter, but robots are able to help.

Phew! It's **hot** in here!

Like a big metal spider, the eight-legged bot Dante II visits active volcanoes to keep track of what is happening inside. It climbs into the crater of the volcano, bringing back samples of gas for scientists to study.

I go where people can't!

Six-legged robot Latro crawls into nuclear storage bases to clear away the harmful waste. If people tried to do the same thing they would be exposed to dangerous levels of radiation.

### Did you know?
Latro moves along on six legs. It carries waste with its two large grippers.

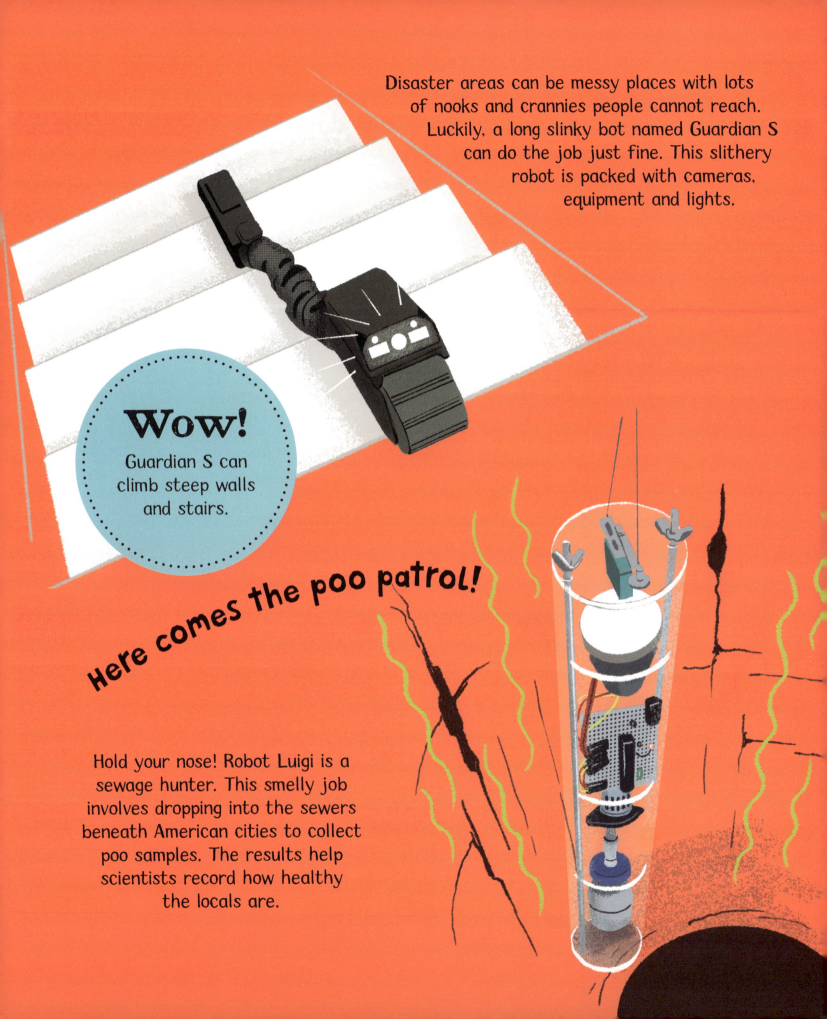

Disaster areas can be messy places with lots of nooks and crannies people cannot reach. Luckily, a long slinky bot named Guardian S can do the job just fine. This slithery robot is packed with cameras, equipment and lights.

## Wow!
Guardian S can climb steep walls and stairs.

## Here comes the poo patrol!

Hold your nose! Robot Luigi is a sewage hunter. This smelly job involves dropping into the sewers beneath American cities to collect poo samples. The results help scientists record how healthy the locals are.

# Out of this world!

**Robots are all over planet Earth — and some even go into space!**

Sending people into space is a risky business. Robots can explore safely and stay longer without any danger to human life. The first robot in space was satellite Sputnik 1. Launched by the Soviet Union in 1957, this battery-powered bot travelled around Earth, sending back data about the atmosphere around our planet.

### Did you know?
Sputnik 1 was about the same size as a bouncy beach ball.

*Time for a moon walk!*

History was made in 1969 when the Apollo 11 astronauts landed on the Moon. Before humans made the trip, various robotic spacecraft visited the Moon. The Lunar Orbiter and Ranger took pictures, while Surveyor brought back samples from the Moon's surface.

### Wow!
Surveyor checked whether a manned spacecraft would be able to land on the Moon.

Most visitors to space are robotic probes and landers designed to carry equipment, so very few look like people! Robonaut 2 is the first humanoid robot to leave our planet. Since 2011 it has been on board the International Space Station, providing a pair of extra hands for the scientists on board.

## Did you know?

Robonaut 2 brings sparkle to space with a glittering golden backpack and matching helmet!

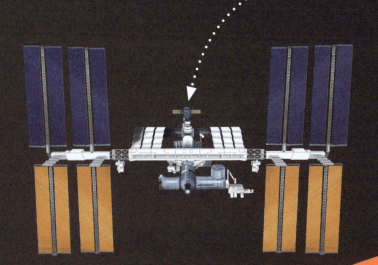

*Hello down there!*

Mars 2020 is a robotic rover built to explore mighty Mars. It will explore the surface, looking for signs that there was once life on Mars.

*I'm looking for signs of life.*

# Artificial intelligence

Robots may appear to be clever clogs, but their brains really come from the brilliant bods who make them.

The brains behind robots are roboticists. They design, build and program robots. Artificial intelligence, or AI, refers to the most clever robots. Their advanced computer programs are designed to copy human intelligence.

High five!

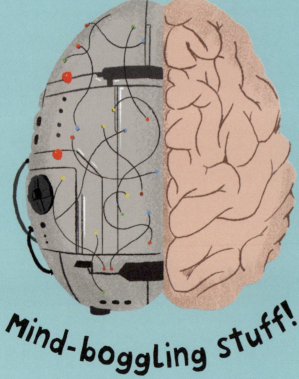

Mind-boggling stuff!

The brain is our body's control centre. For robots, the 'brain' is a computer program created by the roboticist. The program is packed with information. Special software is added so that these robots can behave, interact and make decisions, just like we do.

### Did you know?

The study of robots is called robotics.

# Here are some AI robot examples...

**Face recognition software**
You walk in the room and your robot recognises you and gives you a personal welcome.

*Hello Johnny, how was your day?*

## Wow!
AI robots can learn and remember new things along the way, building up their robot knowledge.

*Bad move, what are you playing at?*

**Computer game skills**
You play a game against your robot and it lets you know when you make a wrong move.

*I'm not surprised you got wet - the weather forecast showed rain!*

**Chatbot software**
You make conversation with your robot and it responds just like a friend.

Robots can be programmed to think, but they are not able to feel emotions naturally like you do. Things like sneezing or yawning also don't come easy to robots. We do them without thinking, but a robot would have to be programmed to copy this behaviour.

*Achoo!*

# Animal instincts

Whether jumping, flying, running or swimming, animal robots move like creatures we know and love.

Animals can feature anything from fur and fuzz to fins and feathers. Robots can be designed to share these looks. Roboticists also study the way animals move and adapt their robots to copy these movements.

*Let's see how fast you can run...*

### Did you know?
Robots that look and behave like animals are called biomimetic robots.

Snakebot is a robot without legs that moves smoothly and speedily, like a snake. It helps find survivors after earthquakes.

*Booooiiiinnnnnng!*

*Slither... slither... slither...*

BionicKangaroo is a robot that jumps and hops around like a kangaroo.

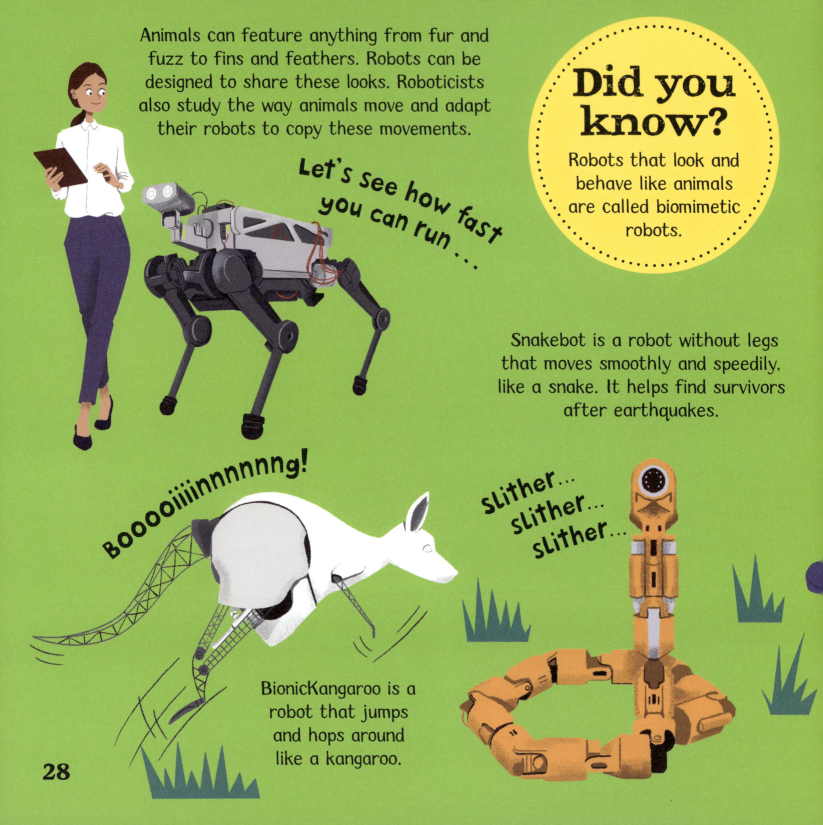

Paro is a seal robot that has all the cuteness of a real seal. Elderly or sick people can stroke Paro's soft fuzz to help them feel better.

Ahhhh!

Flap flap!

eMotionButterfly is a battery-charged butterfly bot that can fly at 9 kilometres per hour!

Here, boy, fetch!

Octobot is a soft bot with no skeleton, just like a real octopus.

That's a lot of arms!

MiRo is a dog bot, designed for children and older people who are unable to have a real dog of their own. MiRo can wag its tail and blink.

Salamandra Robotica II can travel on both land and water in the same way as a salamander. It can swim, walk and crawl, and be used in search and rescue missions.

Make way! Coming through!

# Familiar faces

Who does this remind you of? Does that bot look a bit like you? Say hello to the humanoids!

Humanoid robots usually have a head, arms and legs – the same as you! Not only do they look like us, but they are programmed to behave and respond in a similar way, too.

## Did you know?

An android is a humanoid robot that looks like a man, while a gynoid looks like a woman.

Here I go!

GOAL!!!

Amazing ASIMO was the first robot to walk on two legs, but it can also do much more. ASIMO recognises different objects, understands voice commands and responds to hello handshakes and waves goodbye. It also dances and plays football!

Sophia is the superstar of humanoid robots. She looks very like a real person, with 50 different facial expressions, the ability to have a conversation and a sense of humour that makes everyone laugh!

I have my own passport!

"Uncanny valley" describes the feeling some people get when they find humanoid robots creepy! If you're one of them, don't worry. Humanoids will never properly replace humans because they still have to be programmed by experts to do anything – people are always in control.

## Wow!

Italian painter Leonardo da Vinci sketched ideas for the first humanoid in the 15th century. His design featured a moving suit of armour!

We're not as similar as we look!

# Robots rule

Robots have come far in the past 100 years. Just imagine what they might be able to do in the future...

Like people, robots can be trained to learn a set of instructions for controlling aircraft, trains and cars. They could soon be in the driver's seat!

*My eyes are on the skies!*

*Let's all Learn together!*

Would your school be more fun with robot teachers? Robots have already been taken into schools in the UK to teach children about recycling waste. One day perhaps they will cover all school subjects.

Nanorobots are the teeniest, tiniest technology ever! These super-small robots are being designed to enter the human body and swim through the bloodstream, fixing any health problems.

*Keeping you healthy from the inside out!*